LISTENING TO CASSANDRA

*Making Humanitarian Decision
Making More Effective*

Dennis J. King

Copyright © 2026 by Dennis J. King

All rights reserved.

No part of this book may be reproduced, distributed, or transmitted in any form or by any means, including photocopying, recording, or other electronic or mechanical methods, without the prior written permission of the author, except in the case of brief quotations embodied in critical reviews and certain other noncommercial uses permitted by copyright law.

TABLE OF CONTENTS

Abstract i

Preface iv

Chapter 1: Understanding Humanitarian Decision Making 1

Chapter 2: Three Types Of Decision Making: Strategic/Policy, Programmatic/Funding, Operational/Response 6

Chapter 3: Case Studies On Strategic/Policy, Programmatic/Funding, And Operational/Response Decision Making 13

Chapter 4: Influencing Humanitarian Decision Making 18

Chapter 5: The Science Of Humanitarian Intelligence 24

Chapter 6: The Art Of Humanitarian Intelligence 30

Chapter 7: IA And AI: Intelligent Analyst And Artificial Intelligence 37

Chapter 8: Dennis King's Ten Tips On Writing Effective Humanitarian Intelligence 43

Chapter 9: Anticipating Humanitarian Crises And Challenges 45

Chapter 10: Case Studies On Surprise Events 50

Chapter 11: Making The Humanitarian System Smarter 56

Chapter 12: Recommendations For The Analyst And Decision Maker 62

Appendix 1: Analysis Of Survey Analysis 67

Appendix 2: The Humanitarian Accidental Tourist 73

Index 78

About The Author 80

ABSTRACT

Never has the international humanitarian community had more collective data and information, the most advanced technology, and the most experienced professional workforce than right now.

So why do governments and humanitarian organizations

- still make stupid and ill-informed operational, programmatic, and strategic decisions?
- remain unprepared for surprise emergency events, situations, and unexpected circumstances?
- fail to recognize game-changers and the need to adapt, redesign and restructure the status quo system?

Bottom Line Up Front: The solution to making humanitarian decision making more effective is not new technology, more data and information, or the latest project platforms – it is a trusted analyst or team providing better critical and creative actionable analysis tailored to the decision maker who can be held accountable.

In my over thirty years working in the humanitarian sector for UN agencies and the U.S. Government, I have provided data, information and analysis directly for humanitarian decision makers at **strategic, programmatic and operational** levels. This experience, along with my own personal judgments and proposals, motivated me to write the following document. I am now retired, writing for myself, not affiliated with any group, and free to write from my own personal experience and perspective.

In the first chapter, I explain the often-misunderstood dynamics of humanitarian decision-making based on my experience as a humanitarian affairs analyst, as well as on **surveys and interviews** I conducted with decision makers who work for the UN, Governments, and NGOs.

Chapter 2 delves into three types of humanitarian decision making: **1) Strategic and Policy 2) Programmatic and Funding 3) Operational and Response.**

In the third chapter, I provide **case studies** on each of the three types of humanitarian decision making based on interviews and research.

The fourth chapter explores ways of **influencing decision making** to make it more effective and turning humanitarian analysis into actionable intelligence.

Chapter 5 is an examination of different **types, techniques and disciplines** of humanitarian intelligence.

In the sixth chapter, I assert that humanitarian analysis is **as much an art as it is a science** and I examine the different ways it can be conveyed to decision makers.

Chapter 7 expounds on the **differences between intelligent human analysts and Artificial Intelligence** in assisting humanitarian decision making and how they can complement each other.

Chapter 8 is based on over 30 years in positions providing humanitarian information and analysis and I provide my own **tips on writing effective humanitarian analysis.**

In Chapter 9, I discuss some of the **conceptions and challenges** of unexpected humanitarian crises and disasters that take the international community by surprise.

Chapter 10 is a partial listing of recent (2020 – 25) humanitarian **disasters and disruptions** for which the humanitarian community was not prepared.

In Chapter 11, I explore methods and mechanisms in **making the humanitarian system smarter**, both at the national and international level.

Finally, in Chapter 12, I provide **recommendations** for the humanitarian analyst and for the humanitarian decision maker.

PREFACE

According to ancient Greek mythology and literature, Cassandra was the Trojan princess and daughter of King Priam and was wooed and given the gift of prophecy by the god Apollo. When she rejected his sexual advances, Apollo turned the gift into a curse, so that her prophecies would not be believed, including her warning that the Greeks would destroy the ancient city of Troy. She was considered crazy by her fellow Trojans and was incarcerated by her father Priam. After the fall and destruction of Troy, she was captured and raped by the Greek soldier Ajax and later killed by the Greeks. It did not end well for her.

In the 2017 book **"Warnings: Finding Cassandras to Stop Catastrophes"**, former U.S. Government official Richard A. Clarke and R.P Eddy profile ten individuals who made warnings that went unheeded about eventual disasters and crises, including 2005 Hurricane Katrina, the 2009 Swine flu pandemic, the 2011 Fukushima Nuclear Disaster, the 2011 Arab Spring, and the 2013 Chelyabinsk Siberia meteor strike.

This document is a follow up to the 60-page published research monograph I wrote during a one-year academic sabbatical to the National Intelligence University 2022 – 2023 - **"Channeling Cassandra: Humanitarian Intelligence and Decision making in the Age of Complexity."** That document, using a Complexity Theory conceptual framework, examined the neglected value of applying intelligence techniques, technological tools, and new ways of thinking to address the increasingly complex challenges to humanitarian decision making. Since its publication, the humanitarian universe has become far more complex and even chaotic.

This document offers a more in-depth understanding of the **mysterious process of humanitarian decision making** and gives practical recommendations to make humanitarian analysis and decision making more effective. It is based on my over thirty years of experience in the humanitarian sector, working for the U.S. Agency for International Development, the UN Office for Coordination of Humanitarian Affairs, UNICEF and the US Department of State's Bureau of Intelligence and Research (INR). After 20 years I retired from State/INR in May 2024 and now can write without going through the U.S. Government coordination/clearance process.

Writing this document is on my post-retirement bucket list and it is my attempt to document the practical lessons learned, best practices and personal insights from my experience as a humanitarian affairs analyst. It is my attempt to provide some practical recommendations to make both humanitarian analysis and decision making more effective and counter any reputation I might have as a hopeless Cassandra or "Denny Downer."

READINGS AND REFERENCES

Richard A. Clarke and R.P Eddy. **Warnings: Finding Cassandras to Stop Catastrophes**. Ecco, May 2017. https://www.amazon.com/Warnings-Finding-Cassandras-Stop-Catastrophes/dp/0062488023

Dennis King, **Channeling Cassandra: Humanitarian Intelligence and Decision making in the Age of Complexity**. National Intelligence University, November 2024 https://www.ni-u.edu/wp-content/uploads/2024/11/NIUMonographKing2024_DNI_2024_04334.pdf

CHAPTER 1
Understanding Humanitarian Decision Making

Introduction

Understanding how individuals, groups, or organizations make decisions is always difficult – **decision makers rarely explain how they derive at their decisions**. Some rely on instinct, intuition and accumulated knowledge, especially when decisions are needed quickly. Others go through a procedural process of reviewing as much information and analysis as they can, evaluating it, selecting priorities, identifying options, and finally making the most optimal decision. Another model is brainstorming where a decision maker or group committee identify alternative decisions to make, develop scenarios for each decision action and qualitative and quantitative indicators of success or failure, and imagine unforeseen consequences, potential obstacles and threats.

All actors in a humanitarian crisis make decisions. The **survivors** must make decisions about where to find and receive assistance to meet their immediate needs (food, shelter, medical care, protection, etc.). The **local and national responders** must decide how they can respond and aid the affected populations and what outside assistance is needed. **International humanitarian organizations and donors** must decide which programs to develop and support to address the unmet needs of the crisis-affected populations and return to normalcy and stability.

Challenges

The biggest misunderstanding about humanitarian decision making is the assumption about what decision makers need and instead provide information and analysis based on supply rather than need. Just as we do in deciding what supplies, programs and services to provide to a population in need, the first step is to **assess what analysis for decision making is actually needed** instead of just providing what the organization has in supply.

To find out what decision makers consider as the primary challenges to making decisions – I developed **a survey** sent to individuals who have current or previous humanitarian decision making roles working for the United Nations, government donors, NGOs, etc. Over 35 individuals responded and selected the top five challenges to make humanitarian decisions.

- **Bias (politicization, confirmation, groupthink)** – judgments made in advance due to political agendas, group conformity, or telling the decision maker what they desire to hear.

- **Knowledge Gaps and Unknowns** – lack of access to crisis-affected areas, unanticipated events or situational changes, unavailable tacit knowledge or covert planning

- **Overload** – at the same time there are gaps in the information that decision makers need to know, there is also an overload of information for decision makers to digest. This makes it difficult to find the critical information that is needed.

- **Siloed or status quo thinking** – analysis for decision making is often compartmentalized, disconnected, and lacks alternative perspectives. It perpetuates and preserves the status quo bureaucracy.

- **Lack of actionable information/early warning** – analysis that simply adds knowledge, but does not enhance understanding, anticipate changes, evaluate actions.

Challenges to using analysis for decision making

Challenge	Ranking
Bias (politicization, confirmation, groupthink)	69%
Knowledge Gaps and Unknowns	62%
Overload	56%
Siloed, circular or status quo thinking	50%
Not actionable - not provided in time to act upon	50%
Out-of-Date	44%
Lack of early warning-anticipation	28%
Can't verify or trust source	28%
Misinformation/Disinformation	22%
Conflicting analysis	22%

*See Appendix Analysis of Survey Analysis

Decision Making Pressures

In addition to these challenges, the decision maker faces pressures.

- **Time urgency** – decision makers often must make decisions quickly to save more lives, reduce suffering, and take advantage of opportunities to enhance long-term stability and human security.

- **Known and Unknown Unknowns** – given the dynamic and chaotic parameters of crises, much evidential information is unavailable, out of date, false, or simply not knowable.

- **Paralysis by Analysis** – decision makers become paralyzed and struggle to decide an action due to excessive information and overwhelming choices.

- **Political pressures** – the organization's ideology, self-interests, and power dynamics often drive decision making.

- **Advocacy/media effect** – decision makers can feel pressure from disproportionate media coverage and pro-active advocacy campaigns that can raise awareness about some disaster/crises but may cause others to be neglected.

- **Prioritization** – there are increasing number of people and crises that are in severe life-threatening criticality that require assistance. Diverting food from hungry to feed the starving.

- **Limited resources** – there is a limited and decreasing availability of humanitarian supplies, services, and resources

- **Social media/public awareness** – transparent decision making allows external criticism, challenges, reprisals

- **High Risk** – crisis situations are mostly uncontrollable, so risks and obstacles to effectiveness are more problematic

- **Audit evaluation** – the prospect of financial accountability audit and evaluation inhibits risk taking and commitments when faced with incomplete metrics and uncertainty

The Cynefin framework: Complicated, Complex, Chaos

The Cynefin framework is a conceptual framework used in understanding decision making by categorizing situations into distinct domains. Humanitarian crises can be categorized into three domains, each with different dynamics and challenges for decision making: Complicated, Complex, Chaos.

Complicated – Disasters and crises that are manageable, have a clear cause and effect relationship and follow a linear or cyclical timeline. In these situations, the decision maker analyzes the known facts, assesses the known unknowns, and applies an appropriate tested response.

Complex - this type of humanitarian situation is more complicated than "complicated". Crises emerge from a combination of conditions, drivers, catalysts and triggers rather than from a single cause. Obstacles, challenges, and unexpected circumstances emerge that undermine decisions and actions.

Chaos – a chaotic humanitarian crisis is more complex than "complex", and is marked by greater uncertainty, unpredictability, and moral relativism. There are many "unknown unknowns" and most factors are outside the control of a single humanitarian actor.

READINGS AND REFERENCES

The Cynefin Company, **The Cynefin Framework**, 2005. https://thecynefin.co/about-us/about-cynefin-framework/

CHAPTER 2
Three Types of Decision Making: Strategic/Policy, Programmatic/Funding, Operational/Response

Humanitarian responders, service providers, implementing agencies and donors engage in three types of decision-making:

Strategic/Policy

Strategic/Policy - Headquarters-level policymakers are responsible for strategy and policy development, anticipatory preparedness, and geopolitical diplomatic coordination. This type of analysis and decision-making is centered on advancing the relief organizations' policy goals and countering threats, risks, and adverse actors that oppose or interfere with these goals.

Sample Strategic Decision-making Questions

- *What are the strategies and policies to support to achieve long-term goals?*

- *What advocacy, diplomacy, and coordination actions can address the needs of the crisis-affected populations and counteract any risks, threats, and malign actors during the crisis?*

- *What policies, programs, and opportunities should be supported to address anticipated needs and strategic interests?*

- *When and under what conditions should organizational programs and projects end or be turned over to national and local entities?*

- *What policy and program opportunities can be taken to avert or mitigate the humanitarian effects of anticipated crises or disasters?*

- *What new developments (new actors, new technologies, new approaches, and new threats) could impact the humanitarian system?*

- *What policies and actions would promote local and national resilience, early recovery, and long- term self-sufficiency?*

- *How do humanitarian action and policy interact with development aid, human rights, conflict prevention, conflict resolution, and peacekeeping agendas?*

- *What future threats and challenges will aid organizations need to prepare for?*

- *What are the post-crisis scenarios and plans for stabilization and recovery?*

Time frame: Medium – Long Term

Information needed

- Coordination partners
- Short-term and long-term anticipatory scenarios
- Probability and level of confidence judgments
- Evaluative indicators of success or failure
- Classified intelligence (HUMINT, SIGINT, GEOINT)

Risk/threat assessment

- Malign actors
- Obstruction, sabotage, manipulation
- Unpredictable events, unknown unknowns
- Unforeseen consequences
- Backlash

Post-action Considerations

- Economic Sustainability
- Empowerment and Independence
- Peace and political stability
- Human rights and security
- Timeline and Exit strategy

Programmatic/Funding

Programmatic/Funding - Headquarters-based or Country Mission directors and program and desk officers are responsible for operational planning, program design, resource allocation, project implementation, coordination, and situational monitoring of new and ongoing humanitarian emergencies. Humanitarian actors develop project proposals and program plans for funding and implementation.

Sample Programming Decision-making Questions

- *What are the partner organization projects to develop or fund to address needs of disaster/crisis affected populations?*

- *How bad are the latest severity indicators (deaths, damage, displacement, and so forth) compared to current and past crises?*

- *What are the long-term unmet needs and obstacles related to this disaster or crisis that will need to be addressed?*

- *What are the components of the program (commodities, personnel, permissions, partners, etc.) and what is the timeframe for this assistance?*

- *When, where, and why did people move to escape the crisis situation?*

- *How effective are the national government and local civil society groups who are responding to this disaster? Which organizations are best to work with or support?*

- *What assistance are other donors, international organizations, and NGOs providing for this crisis?*

- *What are their capabilities and motivations?*

- *How does coordination take place?*

Time frame: Medium – Long Term

Information needed

- Most recent population humanitarian needs assessments
- Who's doing what where
- Coordination partners
- Monitoring & Evaluation
- Previous lessons learned/best practices
- Program Proposals and plans

Risk/threat assessment

- Affected target population cooperation
- Diversions and bureaucratic corruption
- Humanitarian access and roadblocks
- Security/safety situation for on-site aid workers
- Local hire drain
- Disrupted resource input

Post-action Considerations

- Timeline and Exit strategy
- Localization empowerment and self-reliance
- Long term recovery and reconstruction
- After action evaluation (lessons learned/best practices)
- Refugee/IDP return and resettlement

Operational/Response

Operational/Response- At the field level of a disaster site, volunteers within the affected community, first responders deployed by the national and other governments, local NGOs, and, sometimes, donors are the first to rescue and tend to survivors. They undertake tactical response activities, including search and rescue, emergency medical care, logistics, temporary shelter, and damage assessment. These first responders are in direct contact with the affected population, applying first-aid, and providing help to those affected.

Sample Response Decision-making Questions

- *What and where are the highest priorities, unaddressed lifesaving needs and opportunities?*

- *Where should we provide emergency assistance to newly affected populations?*

- *What are the most effective means to deliver and distribute aid supplies and services to the affected population?*

- *What are the baseline data indicators for the country or area (for example, population demographics and health, infrastructure) before the emergency—to provide a measure with which to evaluate the change in conditions?*

- *What are the risks, threats, and constraints that humanitarian workers will face in the crisis- affected area?*

- *What are the best ways to counteract the logistical bottlenecks, bureaucratic obstacles, and environmental constraints that hinder fast-and-effective delivery of humanitarian supplies, services, and projects?*

- *What are the best ways to protect critical infrastructure and aid resources at risk during a disaster or conflict?*

Time frame: Immediate – Short-term

Information needed

- Affected target population estimates
- Baseline demographic data
- Assessment of population humanitarian needs
- Baseline GIS map and recent satellite or drone imagery
- Latest situational awareness (social media, texting, etc.)

- Recent on-site situation reporting
- Local response capacity
- Who's doing what where

Risk/threat assessment

- Humanitarian access and roadblocks
- Security/safety situation for on-site aid workers
- Immediate future weather and environmental constraints
- Bureaucratic obstacles
- Unexpected circumstances

Post action Considerations

- Timeline and Exit strategy
- Localization empowerment and resilience
- Restoration of livelihoods
- Follow up recovery and rehabilitation projects

READINGS AND REFERENCES

UN Office for Coordination of Humanitarian Affairs. **Humanitarian Programme Cycle: Step by Step Guide,** May 2022. **https://www.unocha.org/publications/report/world/01-step-step-guide-humanitarian-programme-cycle-2023-may-2022**

Drew Company, **Organizational Levels: Differences and Functions.** 5 June 2023. **https://blog.wearedrew.co/en/concepts/organizational-levels-differences-and-functions**

CHAPTER 3
Case Studies on Strategic/Policy, Programmatic/Funding, And Operational/Response Decision Making

Case Study – Strategic/Policy Decision making: Failure of Diplomacy and Intelligence in forestalling famine – Yemen 2016 – 2021 and Gaza 2023 - 2025

Despite having open-source information, confirmed by U.S. intelligence, about the mass civilian casualties and the worsening humanitarian conditions, four different U.S. administrations chose to pursue a strategy of "quiet diplomacy" that failed to restrain the massive collateral damage actions of the U.S. allies (Saudi-Emirati Coalition and Israel). A U.S. strategy of joining international public condemnation and reducing U.S. arm sales to these allies might have been far more effective in restraining their military actions that directly led to mass civilian casualties, as well as catastrophic malnutrition and starvation, and disease outbreaks that killed thousands more.

In Yemen, the U.S.-backed Saudi-Emirati military Coalition launched a devastating air bombing campaign, with U.S.-supplied bombs and U.S. trained pilots, to attack the Iranian-backed Houthi militants. However, aerial bombing also struck far too many relief clinics, water and sanitation infrastructure, vital humanitarian supply routes and ports, and civilian social gatherings. While the Houthi militants bear responsibility for starting the conflict and obstructing humanitarian access and personnel, the Saudi-Emirati military Coalition was primarily responsible for aggravating the underlying conditions that accelerated a Phase 4 Humanitarian food emergency, exacerbated the spread of cholera, and caused over 20 million people (80% of the population) to require critical humanitarian assistance.

From 2015 to 2016, the Obama administration pursued a policy of quiet engagement, sharing intelligence, and providing support and guidance to the Coalition to try to reduce attacks on civilian targets, but this approach failed to hinder their reckless bombing campaign and disregard for civilian casualties. Starting in 2017, the Trump administration provided even more political and military support and reduced U.S. Government diplomatic pressure on the Coalition.

In Gaza in 2023 - 24, U.S. administration failed to take action that would have put significant pressure on Israel to stop obstructing delivery of humanitarian aid to 2.2 million starving and forcibly displaced Gazans. Under the terms of the 1995 Congressionally passed Humanitarian Aid Corridor Act - Section 620I of the Foreign Assistance Act, foreign assistance and arm sales are prohibited from being made available to any country whose government restricts the transport or delivery of U.S. humanitarian assistance. However, the Biden administration waived the Act under the stipulation of national security and the Government of Israel continued to bomb civilian areas, forcibly displace Gazans and block the transport of life-saving humanitarian supplies through Israeli controlled border crossings into the Gaza Strip.

The U.S. had little direct influence on the perpetrator of the triggering October 7 attack, Hamas, which by October 2025 still held 20 Israeli hostages out the of 250 abducted and held in captivity. The others had been previously released in exchanges between Israel and

Hamas or were killed or died during captivity in Gaza. Finally on 13 October 2025, after two years, there was an agreement as a result of Qatari, Egyptian and Turkish pressure on the remaining Hamas leadership to return the 20 hostages to Israel. Following the release of the 20 hostages, Israel agreed to open more cross-border and internal humanitarian access to UN agencies and some humanitarian NGOs to deliver and distribute life-saving supplies.

These two cases dramatically illustrate how available information and intelligence and a quiet diplomacy approach do not necessarily lead to decisions that reduce human suffering in foreign humanitarian crises. In both cases, consideration of domestic political pressures and motivation to counteract Iran's and other rival's influence in the region overruled a **humanitarian-driven strategy**. Threatening to reduce arms sales to these allies and publicly condemning their war crimes may have applied the necessary pressure to motivate them to adjust their military strategies to avoid inflicting massive civilian casualties and exacerbating humanitarian impacts.

Input provided by Jeremy Konyndck, Director of USAID Office of Foreign Disaster Assistance (2013–2017) and current President of Refugees International since 2023.

Case study – Programmatic Decision-Making: OCHA's Country Based Pooled Funds (CBPF)

CBPFs are established when an emergency occurs or when an existing crisis deteriorates, and are managed by OCHA, led by the UN Resident Coordinators (RCs) in close coordination with the humanitarian community. Life-saving projects by local and national actors are favored, as these actors typically are best placed to provide front-line services due to their proximity to the affected communities, their local knowledge, linkages with local authorities and community acceptance.

Before being eligible to submit project proposals for funding, all prospective non-governmental organization partners are screened and vetted, then registered in the UN Partner Grant Management Systems and undergo due diligent review and capacity assessment. Partner organizations must also adhere to humanitarian values, including protection from sexual exploitation and abuse. Decisions on which project proposals to fund are based on the UN Humanitarian Response Plans, on-going needs and risks assessments, and facilitated by field surveys, AI tools, and consultation with the affected populations.

Source: UN Office for the Coordination of Humanitarian Affairs, Financing and Outreach Division

Case Study – Operational Decision-Making: Aid Worker Security in Iraq

Abby Stoddard relates a recent example from Iraq where a data firehose of incident reports, supplied by an international security consortium, created paralysis among some security people working for NGOs. "They couldn't sift through it all to see what a major threat was and what wasn't. This added to the overtly restrictive approach that the humanitarian community was taking. Conversely, when the security monitoring system was shut down by the government for a period of some months and there was no data feed of incidents at all, NGOs were also scrambling and felt they were flying blind." Example of both **paralysis by analysis** and **knowledge gaps**.

Abby Stoddard is founder/partner of Humanitarian Outcomes and contributed input.

READINGS AND REFERENCES

Jeremy Konyndyk, **The Humanitarian Crisis in Yemen: Addressing Current Political and Humanitarian Challenges,** Testimony before House Committee on Foreign Affairs, 6 March 2019

Signatories. **An Open Statement on Yemen**. 11 November 2018.https://www.justsecurity.org/wp-content/uploads/2021/01/yemen-statement-former-obama-officials-november-11-2018.pdf

Humanitarian Aid Corridor Act - S.230,104th Congress (1995-1996) https://www.congress.gov/bill/104th-congress/senate-bill/230

Akbar Shadid Ahmed, **Biden Discussed Potential Israeli War Crimes In Gaza. He Kicked The Can To Trump.** HuffPost, 7 Nov 2025. **https://www.huffpost.com/entry/biden-intelligence-israeli-war-crimes-gaza_n_690e361ce4b0dd4ea75b6445?2b9**

UN Office for Coordination of Humanitarian Affairs (OCHA), **Country Based Pooled Funds Guidelines**, 3 May 2023. https://www.unocha.org/publications/report/world/country-based-pooled-funds-global-guidelines-enar

CHAPTER 4
Influencing Humanitarian Decision Making

Stoic Dichotomy of Control

Humanitarian decision making often involves crises, disasters, and situations that are outside the control of a single humanitarian actor. Ancient Greek Roman Stoic philosophy divides events and situations into those that are within our control and those that are not. In the field of humanitarian action and decision making, it is important to recognize this distinction. While there are long-term, big-picture strategic goals that humanitarian actors can aspire to, there are more realistic pragmatic objectives and outcomes that humanitarian actors can hope to influence and achieve.

The first step is to recognize and acknowledge what events and situations you can have influence on, and which ones are outside your control. Of course, you can still make decisions and take actions that address the uncontrollable events and situations, but you should manage expectations.

However, humanitarian actors should not make decisions and take actions in pursuit of objectives or outcomes that undermine the overriding strategic goal. While taking an action or making a statement may make the actor feel they are following a moral principle, it can be counter-productive to achieving the strategic goal that is in the best of interest of the affected population in the long-run.

Lack of Control ↑

STRATEGIC GOALS

CONDITIONS, INDICATORS, OBSTACLES

OBJECTIVES, OUTCOMES

ACTVITIES, ACTIONS, ASSUMPTIONS, DECISIONS

↓ More Control

Humanitarian Intelligence

As someone who worked both for the humanitarian community and the U.S. intelligence community, the word "intelligence" was perceived as a dirty word by many humanitarian professionals. Usually equated with spying, covert action, non-transparency and arrogance, intelligence can also be defined as **actionable analysis**. It is not enough to simply make analysis available; it should be made useful for making decisions. The term Artificial Intelligence (or as I sometimes call it "**dehumanized Intelligence**") is promoted and much more accepted by the humanitarian community.

Humanitarian intelligence should answer the questions that **decision makers want to know but they also need to know**. It should not simply give an answer that the decision maker wants to hear, but provide objective analysis, challenge assumptions, and make judgments when information is not perfect. In this time of misinformation, disinformation and malign actions, humanitarian intelligence is needed to provide humanitarian actors with the best analysis for making decisions. By intelligence, I do not mean just declassified intelligence derived from "national technical means", but also the vast amount of open-source intelligence that is not classified.

Case Studies: Intelligence success and failures: Ukraine 2022 and Gaza 2023

In the months prior to the full-scale Russian invasion of Ukraine in February 2022, the U.S. and U.K governments declassified and released its high-resolution satellite imagery and selected SIGINT intercepts to counteract Russian disinformation and provide evidence of Russian planning and military build-up to launch a massive invasion of Ukraine. Given the U.S. intelligence failure regarding WMD in Iraq, some humanitarian organizations were skeptical and considered the Russian military build-up as a bluff. However, others did make contingency plans and augmented their European stockpiles in preparation for this scenario, which turned out to be true and worse than they conceived.

On 7 October 2023, Hamas launched rocket attacks and a cross-border incursion of Israel that killed 1,200 people in Israel and abducted 250 more as hostages taken back to the Gaza Strip. The failure for Israeli and U.S. intelligence to anticipate the worst attack on Israel in its history was the result of several causes. Israeli intelligence overconfidence, groupthink, failure of underground, overhead and communication sensors, the lack of HUMINT inside Gaza, and failure to implement countermeasures resulted in the Israeli military being taken completely by surprise. However, perhaps even more significant was Hamas' total control over journalists and humanitarian aid workers inside Gaza, including UNRWA, making them unable or reluctant to report on suspicious activities such as tunneling, Hamas co-locating in hospitals and schools, and training rehearsals.

Humanitarian Diplomacy

Humanitarian diplomacy is the use of high-level engagement to influence parties to armed conflicts and their sponsors to pursue humanitarian objectives. Examples of humanitarian diplomacy include

- Prevent and subvert planned actions that will create humanitarian crises
- Negotiate humanitarian access with armed groups
- Anticipate the actions of participants in the humanitarian crisis
- Understand the needs, motivations and objectives of other humanitarian actors
- Persuade, pressure, and influence other actors in achieving your humanitarian objectives
- Prepare for and overcome the obstacles, malign actions, the sabotage planned by other actors during the humanitarian crisis.

To be effective, humanitarian diplomacy must often be done "quietly" and use "inside information" that may need to be strictly controlled, encrypted, and even classified. Transparency and advocacy can be counterproductive to achieving strategic goals, beneficial objectives and successful outcomes. Advocacy, however, can be useful in galvanizing public pressure on other actors to change policies and achieve a specific objective.

The 5 Cs of Humanitarian Effectiveness: Cooperation, Collaboration, Coordination, Constructive, Common Sense

Making a decision that leads to effective humanitarian action depends on five things:

Cooperation: A humanitarian action, program, or service from an external humanitarian actor to an affected population requires the community's acceptance, trust, and helpful participation to succeed.

Collaboration: Separate humanitarian actors benefit from an exchange of information and a shared understanding of the situation and challenges.

Coordination: Humanitarian actions are more likely to be effective if they are implemented in synergistic coordination with complementary activities of different actors that seek the same objective/outcome.

Constructive: Humanitarian actions are more likely to be effective if they serve a useful, positive purpose, and not perfunctory and self-serving.

Common Sense – when perfect data, information, and evidence are not available, effective humanitarian action must rely on intuition, lessons learned and wisdom.

READINGS AND REFERENCES

What is Stoicism.com. **What is the dichotomy of Control?** 13 March 2022 https://whatisstoicism.com/stoicism-definition/what-is-the-dichotomy-of-control

Vince Peeler. **Actionable Intelligence**. Blog Substack, 5 March 2025. https://vincepeeler.substack.com/p/actionable-intelligence

Andrej Zwitter. **Humanitarian Intelligence: A Practitioner's Guide to Crisis Analysis and Project Design.** Rowman & Littlefield, 2016 humanitarianintelligence.net

OCHA on Message: **Humanitarian Diplomacy**, UN Office for the Coordination of Humanitarian Affairs, August 2024 https://www.unocha.org/publications/report/world/ocha-message-humanitarian-diplomacy-august-2024

Jake Harrington. **Intelligence Disclosures in the Ukraine Crisis and Beyond**. War in the Rocks, 22 March 2022. https://warontherocks.com/2022/03/intelligence-disclosures-in-the-ukraine-crisis-and-beyond/

Joshua C. Huminski. **Russia, Ukraine and the Future Use of Strategic Intelligence**. PRISM 10, No.3, 7 September 2023. https://ndupress.ndu.edu/PRISM/PRISM-10 -3/

Francois Grunewald, "**Real-Time Evaluation of the Humanitarian Response to the Crisis Resulting from the War in Ukraine**" *Groupe URD,* "August 28, 2022, https://reliefweb.int/report/ukraine/real-time-evaluation-humanitarian-response-ukraine-july-24th-august-18th-2022

Michel Wyss. **The October 7 Attack: An Assessment of the Intelligence Failings**. Combating Terrorism Center Sentinel. October 2024. **https://ctc.westpoint.edu/october-2024/**

Dennis J. King

CHAPTER 5
The Science of Humanitarian Intelligence

Humanitarian intelligence is not recognized as a professional discipline by the international humanitarian community, nor within the U.S. intelligence community. However, the human impacts of natural disasters, health emergencies and conflict crises can be significant **drivers of political, social, and economic instability** at the national and global levels. Humanitarian intelligence must be **multi-disciplinary**, incorporating the physical sciences, the social sciences, economics, international affairs, logistics, health and medicine.

Humanitarian intelligence disciplines and expertise

- **International affairs** - geopolitical interactions, security, economics, natural resources, conflict, diplomacy, human rights, institutions, nation-states, non-state actors

- **Natural hazards/disasters** – geologic (earthquakes, tsunamis, volcanoes), meteorological (storms, flooding, drought)

- **Climate change** – recent man-made phenomenon of increased global temperature, altering weather patterns and generating more frequent and severe meteorological disasters, as well heat waves, wildfires, sea level rise

- **Environmental** – infestation, oil spills, toxic contamination, pollution/haze, blights, species threats

- **Health and Medicine** – Epidemics, pandemics, child/infant/maternal health, disease, disability or health threats

- **Food security** – agriculture, food shortages, famine, malnutrition

- **Conflict/insecurity** - Armed attacks between nation-states or groups and generalized criminal gang violence

- **Human Rights** - Genocide, atrocities, ethnic cleansing, confinement, abductions, war crimes

- **Displacement** – IDPs due to conflict or disaster, refugee exodus, migration, evacuation, shelter

- **Humanitarian System** - actors, network, mechanisms, technology, aid worker security a

Case Study: Famine Early Warning Systems Network (FEWSNET) and Integrated Food Security Phase Classification (IPC)

The word "famine" has emotional connotations and has often been misused in describing short-term food shortages, drought-induced agricultural failures, chronic malnutrition, and persistent food insecurity to raise alarm about a situation. FEWSNET and the IPC were efforts to establish scientific rigor to describe different levels of food insecurity and provide evidence to inform humanitarian decision making.

In the midst of the Ethiopia famine in 1985, the U.S. Government created the Famine Early Warning System later becoming FEWSNET to provide on-line analysis on food insecurity situations around the world. FEWSNET uses an integrated approach that analyzes meteorological data, agriculture production, market prices, trade, nutrition, coping mechanisms, and local livelihoods to monitor, forecast, warn and anticipate scenarios to inform humanitarian decision makers.

The IPC, first developed in 2004 for Somalia, is a multi-organization collaborative framework for defining five distinct phases of food security assessment – generally food secure, borderline food insecure, acute food and livelihood crisis, humanitarian emergency and famine-humanitarian catastrophe. The system is based on a progressive scale, with quantitative thresholds, scientific methodology, and qualitative indicators including food production, humanitarian access, livelihood sustainability, market supply and demand, etc.

Structured Analytic Techniques

Structured Analytic Techniques (SAT) are systematic exercises used to analyze any issue, diagnose or reframe any problem, support decision-making, and anticipate future events.

Some SATs useful for humanitarian intelligence include

- **Brainstorming** – facilitating a structured group discussion to identify issues, generate ideas, and propose options

- **Devil's Advocacy** – providing an alternative judgment, contrarian viewpoint, or potential fallacies to challenge already presented analysis.

- **Red Team Analysis** - role playing from the point of view of an adversary or potential obstacles

- **Alternative Future Scenarios** – imagining a range of potential future states in situations of high uncertainty.

- **Wind-tunneling** - testing the prospective resilience of a strategy, plan, or program against various future scenarios.

Types of Humanitarian Intelligence

There are several types of intelligence that are applicable to humanitarian analysis and synthesis used to answer key questions of decision makers. These include:

Situational Analysis/Synthesis (What is happening?) examines what is known about humanitarian situations, locations, actors, specific events, etc. Because the humanitarian situation is constantly changing, it needs to be monitored to keep decision makers informed with up-to-date analysis. It can take the format of a situation summary report or a situational visualization that includes graphics, maps, and chronological timelines.

Explanatory Analysis/Synthesis (Why is it happening?) explores the causes, triggers, and factors contributing to a humanitarian crisis or disaster. It might be presented as a written summary document, or a visualized causal map or network chart.

Evaluative Analysis/Synthesis (What are the positive/negative results?) makes judgments about the value and significance of a situation, response, project, etc. After action reports, lessons learned, best practices, and independent evaluation studies of past humanitarian crises are examples of this type of analysis, which can be useful for current decision-making.

Comparative Analysis/Synthesis (How does it compare?) contrasts the similarities, differences, and relative values among two or more humanitarian crises and how they rank against each other. This type of analysis can be in the form of a matrix, index, or map that gives a numerical score or color-coded designation to a list of distinct humanitarian crises, based on core variable indicators.

Estimative/Predictive Analysis/Synthesis (What will be the future events and trends?) identifies, describes, and forecasts events, conditions or probable outcomes that might be expected to exist months and even years ahead. It is usually based on past data and behavioral trends and can use predictive analytics, such as data mining, ML, AI algorithms, and agent-based modeling techniques.

Anticipatory Analysis/Synthesis (What Could Happen?) foresees and warns about emerging conditions, trends, threats, and opportunities that may require a rapid shift in posture, priorities, or preparation. It is more about exploring scenarios and possibilities than predicting the timing of future events.

Crisis Analysis and Project Design

In his 2016 book, *Humanitarian Intelligence: A Practitioner's Guide to Crisis Analysis and Project Design,* University of Groningen Professor Andrej Zwitter states, "Humanitarian intelligence aims to **reduce uncertainty and risk** by providing the basis of informed decision-making. …using investigative and analytical techniques in the service of rapid and continuous assessment, project and program development, impact evaluation and learning."

READINGS AND REFERENCES

Famine Early Warning System**, About FEWSNET**. 2025. https://fews.net

Integrated Food Security Phase Classification (IPC), **About the IPC**. https://www.ipcinfo.org

Richards J. Heuer and Randolph H. Person. **Structured Analytic Techniques for Intelligence Analysis.** Sage, 2015. https://uk.sagepub.com/en-gb/eur/structured-analytic-techniques-for-intelligence-analysis /book255432

Andrej Zwitter, **Humanitarian Intelligence: A Practitioner's Guide to Crisis Analysis and Project Design.** Rowman & Littlefield, 2016. **humanitarianintelligence.net**

Dennis J. King

CHAPTER 6
The Art of Humanitarian Intelligence

Humanitarian intelligence is more than just providing collected data and reported information, it is **as much an art as it is a science**. Making humanitarian information and analysis available does not mean it will be accessed and used for decision making. Faced with an overwhelming amount of analysis and options pushed to them, decision makers will select to read or listen to human analysts that provide unique insight, stimulate their thinking and are trusted based on experience.

The 4 Ps: Preparation, Presentation, Persuasion, Proximity

In addition to subject matter expertise, technical skills and scientific methods, actionable humanitarian intelligence requires "soft skills" such as creative and critical thinking, collaboration, problem solving, and communication skills. I have come up with four Ps to make humanitarian intelligence more effective and actionable.

Preparation – anticipate the questions that the decision maker need answered, provide probability and confidence levels for judgments and predictions. Recognize alternatives, obstacles, challenges, and creative options.

Presentation – provide humanitarian intelligence in a format tailored to the intended audience – written, visual, oral briefing, or interactive presentation.

Persuasion – beyond just presentation and availability, humanitarian intelligence benefits from direct interaction with the intended audience, personal experience storytelling, and easy comprehension.

Proximity – the closer the source of humanitarian intelligence is to both the crisis and to the decision maker, the more influential and effective it can be.

The Power of Presentation

Survey Ranking personal preferences for receiving information /analysis

Format	Ranking
Written	4.47
Visual	4.25
Group Interactive	4.09
Deep Dive briefings	3.78
Personal interactive	3.23
AI Q&A Chatbot	1.31

*See Appendix Analysis of Survey Analysis

Written

Given the limited time and attention span of most decision makers, most of them want their written analysis concise, to the point, and easy to read. These written documents should start with the **Bottom Line Up Front** – the key judgment and takeaway. Written documents can be underlined, highlighted, annotated and referred to later. They can provide context, background, insight, and logic more effectively than visual or oral presentations.

Writing and reading, however are fast becoming a "lost art" in this age of AI, social media, podcasts, and visual dashboards. **People no longer read, they scan**. According to an internal study for UNGA80, only the top five percent of UN reports are downloaded more than 5,500 times, while a staggering 20% receive fewer than 1,000 downloads each year – which are all not necessarily read. The first challenge is getting the document read – *see Chapter 8: Dennis King's tips on writing effective humanitarian intelligence.*

Visual

Decision makers like to have data and information visualized in an infographic, which may be a combination of **charts, graphs, tables, maps and short text boxes** – all on one page, a computer screen. a PPT slide, or on an **interactive dashboard**. However, the graphic should not be too dense, too difficult to view and digest, or too distracting with too many colors, symbols, and different interpretations. Visualizations are simplifications and should recognize disclaimers, caveats, and missing data.

Satellite or drone imagery can be powerful and useful for planning, for documenting impacts, and for before and after assessments of areas that are difficult to access. A trained geo-spatial analyst is necessary to interpret and annotate the photographic product, to make sure images are correctly identified. Photographic imagery is **susceptible to deep fake deception, ambiguity, and misinterpretation.**

Deep Dive briefings

Other decision makers are more responsive to **group oral briefings, presentations or podcasts**. A skilled briefer can weave in personal storytelling, personal rapport with the audience, and a structured persuasive outline. The analyst can highlight the important points. Oral briefings are linear/sequential and cannot be used later, unless memorized, recorded or transcribed. The time duration, agenda, and amount of flexibility tend to be controlled.

Convenient timing and common location are constraints to arranging **in-person, deep dive group briefings**. However, virtual meetings or podcasts can be scheduled for participants in different locations using video meeting applications and webcams. For presentations to large audiences or virtual podcasts, the challenge for the presenter is competing for attention with multi-tasking cell phone surfing.

Group Interactive

Another type of briefing is a more intentionally **interactive meeting or focus group**, where the agreed upon facts of the problem are presented or provided as "backgrounders". Then, representatives from different offices having different perspectives weigh in, and someone serving as facilitator manages the process and tries to reach a consensus on a recommendation for a decision. Some software event management tools, such as Slido, enable some degree of group interaction in virtual settings.

One example of an interactive decision-making meeting/briefing is the **U.S. National Security system**, which involves a hierarchical process of separate committee meetings. First is a convening of experts and analysts at the working level, then filtering of information and options at the deputy senior leadership level. At this level, the analysis is vetted and passed on to discussion by the Principals of Cabinet Secretaries and agency heads, chaired by the National Security Advisor. At the apex, final arguments, options and recommendations are presented to the President for final decision.

Personal interactive

Another type of analysis communication is the in-person, **one-on-one interaction between the decision maker and the analyst/advisor**. The interaction starts with addressing a problem, question or decision that needs to be made, spelling out the key knowns of the situation, the possible unknown unknowns, and allowing for interactive Q&A, challenges, and personal rapport. A well-known example of this is **the Presidential Daily Briefing (PDB)** – a scheduled meeting between the President and senior U.S. intelligence community officials. Various past U.S. Presidents have used the PDB in different formats or not at all.

In fast-onset, dynamic disaster or crisis situations, a **situation room or Op Center** may be set up to serve as a central information hub for collecting, tracking and processing quickly changing situational data and information. This situation room/operation center can be used for time-critical operational response decision making. It is functional 24/7, works best when the crisis management team members are co-located, graphic information is visually displayed, and information can be shared easily to team members for making quick decisions.

AI Chatbot

A recent survey on humanitarians using AI in 2025 found while individual humanitarian workers were embracing AI tools, most larger humanitarian organizations were still in the experimentation phase when adopting its use in operations, programming and policy making. In my own selective survey of humanitarian operational, programmatic and policy decision makers, AI chatbots were usually ranked as the **least preferred way of receiving humanitarian analysis**.

AI tools can be useful when decisions are needed to figure out logistic routes, match needs to supply, answer fact-based questions, evaluate key project performance indicators, etc. However, when decisions are needed that are strategic and policy-oriented and can affect the lives of affected populations, most decision makers prefer to have presented actionable analysis that has been **verified and vetted**, provides **caveats, disclaimers, and retrievable sources**, considers alternatives and unknowns, and can be challenged.

READINGS AND REFERENCES

Bruce E, Pease. **Leading Intelligence Analysis**. Sage, 2020. https://collegepublishing.sagepub.com/products/leading-intelligence-analysis-1- 258717

Michele Nichols. **UN report finds United Nations reports are not widely read**. Reuters, 1 August 2025 https://www.reuters.com/world/un-report-finds-united-nations-reports-are-not-widely-read-2025-08-01/

David Priess. **The US President's daily dose of intelligence**. Engelsberg Ideas, 7 May 2025. https://engelsbergideas.com/essays/the-us-presidents-daily-dose-of-intelligence/

Ka Man Parkinson et al. **Artificial intelligence in the humanitarian sector: mapping current practice and future potential**. Humanitarian Leadership Academy. August 2025, https://www.humanitarianleadershipacademy.org/resources/report-artificial-intelligence-in-the-humanitarian-sector-mapping-current-practice-and-future-potential-august-2025/

Chapter 7
IA and AI: Intelligent Analyst and Artificial Intelligence

It takes an experienced and trained carpenter to properly use the tools available, be aware of the risks and limitations, and add their own unique personal touch to the product. As the saying goes, "it is a poor carpenter who blames his tools." It is the carpenter, not the tool that should receive the appraisal, level of trust and confidence of the user of the product. Once the product is finished, the user evaluates it and decides if it is best to accomplish a specific task. The outcome then becomes the responsibility of the user of the product.

AI should be promoted as a tool and not as a standalone solution. In the promotion of AI, "it" is given credit for saving lives, predicting events, negotiating peace, making decisions, being "good" as if AI is a human being. What is frequently neglected in the promotion of AI is the **role of the humanitarian personnel – the assessment team, the analyst/advisor, the decision maker**. Deep down we all know that the only solution to the toughest problems of humanity is humanity itself.

While I am often impressed with AI's ability to quickly summarize, extract key data, as well as write grammatically and generate conclusions, we humans should not start giving up our ability to think, imagine, write, question, empathize and make judgments and decisions. **We can be easily seduced by AI**. Progress in addressing the most critical humanitarian challenges can only be made by **reinforcing human responsibility for humanity**.

Beware of Geeks bearing gifts

Technology has long played a role in the humanitarian sector: GIS, satellite imagery, internet, social media, smartphones, drones, biometrics, and most recently AI have **revolutionized the humanitarian profession**. Within the international humanitarian community there has emerged a humanitarian technocracy. Technology has come to play an important role in the humanitarian ecosystem.

In recent years, many conferences, summits, UN side events, academic courses, podcasts, blogs, etc. have been organized to promote AI in the humanitarian sector. Some of these are funded and sponsored by the major AI companies. Many of the most pervasive AI tools are developed by either American or Chinese multinational corporations. **AI will perpetuate the digital divide in the humanitarian sector**, used by well-resourced humanitarian organizations headquartered in the Global North, far removed from the crisis-affected countries and populations in the Global South.

In February 2019, the UN World Food Program (WFP) and **Palantir Artificial Intelligence Platform** announced a five-year $45 million partnership aimed at helping WFP use its data to streamline the delivery of food and cash-based assistance in life-saving emergency relief operations around the world. Almost immediately, other humanitarians voiced concern about giving access to WFP internal data to a private company with contracts with U.S. military, the CIA, ICE, the FBI, several local and national police departments, as well as the Israeli and UK governments. In the published WFP Global Artificial Intelligence Strategy 2025-2027, there is no mention of the 5-year partnership with Palantir or a use case evaluation.

Recently, there has been significant promotion of the concept of AI for Good and Humanitarian AI ethics with built-in moral standards and principles. Again, we must not forget that **AI is a tool and only**

as good and ethical as the people who design and use it. AI was used in conceiving, planning and implementing the 2024 U.S. military's Gaza pier project and the 2025 U.S.-Israeli Gaza Humanitarian Foundation program, two efforts that have been recognized as colossal failures. The Israeli Defense Force developed and used an AI tool known as Lavender to identify and target Hamas militants, but it has been reported that it detected at least 10% false positives using biased or incomplete data.

By jumping on the **AI bandwagon**, humanitarian organizations should not give up their ability and responsibility for making decisions and taking actions that save lives, reduce suffering and improve conditions. AI can separate humanitarians from the victims of disasters and crises, the knowledge they need to have, and the connection with humanity. AI can be used to generate its own disinformation, **"deepfakes" and "hallucinations"** that can deceive even other AI systems. It also raises serious data privacy and verification concerns and facilitates uncoordinated analysis and decision making.

Putting the Human back in Humanitarianism

Faced with complexity and chaos, overwhelming overload of data and information, and extreme pressures on the workload of the humanitarian community, it is understandable that decision makers would want and seek easy solutions. However, **just because information and analysis are made available does not mean that it will be used for decision making.** It takes a human analyst to know what the decision maker needs to know, to recommend critical information products to be read, and to understand the unique interests, preferences, and priorities of the decision maker.

Things an Intelligent Analyst can do better than AI

- **The Four Ps** – Influencing humanitarian decision making depends on Preparation, Presentation, Persuasion, Proximity **(See Chapter6)**

- **Accountability** – decision makers must be able to trust the provider of the analysis they use, so that they can accept responsibility for the decisions that they make.

- **Empathy** - to AI, people are just data. Humanitarian values, compassion, and taking risks are not considered in AI-driven humanitarian action decision-making.

- **Tacit Intuition and Wisdom** - Decision making cannot always rely on only empirical evidence, especially in chaotic and uncertain crisis situations. Sometimes, intuition is needed to fill in the gaps. Likewise, wisdom is derived from personal experience.

- **Creative Thinking** - AI modeling is based on what datasets are available (verified or unverified) and past historical precedence and cannot imagine unknown unknowns, unanticipated events, and unforeseen threats and risks.

The Carpenter and the tool

Remember, **AI does not make decisions – team leaders, project managers and policy makers do.**

AI can be useful in

- filtering and extracting data and information for summarized analysis amazingly fast

- answering questions where the facts are known and accessible, quickly and straight forwardly

- determining optimal logistics routes for delivering relief supplies

- matching assessed emergency needs to available humanitarian resources

- evaluating key project performance indicators

- assessing potential areas that might experience natural disasters, epidemics or conflict based on existing on-line historical data, etc.

However, crisis situations are dynamic and collected data and information are often **quickly out of date, unable to be verified, or simply not available**. The actors in a crisis, such as combatants in a conflict, the humanitarian responders, and the affected populations, can make their own decisions and actions that are **not necessarily rational** and therefore not likely to be predicted. **Political leaders can sometimes choose to ignore or deny proven facts and evidence.** AI is not able to address these issues.

My skepticism about the **overpromotion of AI** is not so much a criticism of its capabilities and potential applications, but more a recognition of the neglect of mentioning **the role of the human in humanitarian decision making.** AI is here to stay, but it should not replace the role of the analyst and the decision maker, otherwise we are in danger of becoming totally reliant on it and lose the ability to write, analyze, make decisions, and be accountable for your work.

Like the carpenter and the tool, **the analyst and AI must work together to inform decision making.** Simply generating answers, conclusions, reports and plausible scenarios is not enough - it does not guarantee that the analysis will lead to decisions and actions. It takes a human analyst to cross-check the output from AI, respond to the decisionmaker's challenges, disprove disinformation, justify the analytical judgments, and explain the unknowables to the decision maker.

The trick is getting people to **listen to Cassandras.**

READINGS AND REFERENCES

Dennis King. **2084: the Shape of Things to Come – a short story satire.** LinkedIn, 21 July 2025. https://www.linkedin.com/pulse/2084-shape-things-come-dennis-king-aoqve/

Ethical ai alliance. **Filling the Accountability Gap: Towards a Global Monitoring & Reporting Mechanism for AI Harms.** Policy Brief, September 2025. https://static1.squarespace.com/static/660fed256b381f5933f09fb2/t/68d416e33f8a17306307b14f/1758729955416/EAIA_PolicyBrief_GlobalMRM_AIHarms_FINAL_Sep2025_vSENT.pdf

World Food Programme, **Palantir and WFP partner to help transform global humanitarian delivery,** 5 February 1019, https://www.wfp.org/news/palantir-and-wfp-partner-help-transform-global-humanitarian-delvery

Magan Naidoo. **WFP Global Artificial Intelligence Strategy 2025 – 2027,** World Food Programme, 20 March 2025. https://www.wfp.org/publications/wfp-global-artificial-intelligence-strategy-2025-2027

Faine Greenwood. **Why Humanitarians Are Worried About Palantir's New Partnership With the U.N.** Slate, 12 February 2019, https://slate.com/technology/2019/02/palantir-un-world-food-programme-data-humanitarians.html

Mehul Srivastava and Felicia Schwartz, **How the US's $230mn Gaza pier became a 'colossal failure'.** The Financial Times, 15 July 2024, https://www.ft.com/content/7a56bc4b-d192-4592-8151-0ff943932d82

CHAPTER 8
Dennis King's Ten Tips on Writing Effective Humanitarian Intelligence

1. Come up with a **stimulating, intriguing or self-explanatory title** that makes the reader want to read the piece. If you are reading this, it worked.

2. In the first paragraph of a written analysis, state the **BLUF – Bottom Line Up Front** (does not mean pretending to have information you do not have).

3. Write your analysis to answer a decision maker's question, either requested, implied or unarticulated. **Tell them what they need to know, not what they want to hear.**

4. **Write short articles, documents, and chapters** that are between 800 and 1200 words, paragraphs three to five sentences in length, and able to be read in two to four minutes.

5. To keep the document brief and therefore read, **excise sentences that tell the reader what they already know**, and/or what is not necessary.

6. **People don't read any more - they scan.** Include graphics, **bolded words**, bulletized lists, underlined phrases, text boxes, shortened sentences and paragraphs.

7. Be stylistic to be **memorable and unique** – use metaphors, personalization, verbal imagery, and historical or literary allusions if appropriate.

8. Be sure to provide any necessary **caveats, disclaimers, acknowledged gaps, and source citations** for quoted facts. Convey your level of confidence in your analysis and judgments – high, moderate or low – or your reservations.

9. Don't feel the need to write a lengthy document or **show off your pedantic knowledge** just to please yourself or academics.

10. **Be original and value-added** to stand out amongst the document overload.

READINGS AND REFERENCES

Louis M. Kaiser and Pandolph H. Pherson. **Analytic Writing Guide**. Pherson Associates LLC, 2020, https://www.amazon.com/Analytic-Writing-Guide-Louis-Kaiser/dp/1735655007

Walter Voskian and Randolph H. Pherson. **Analytic Production Guide for Managers of Intelligence and Business Analysts.** Pherson Associates LLC, 2015 https://www.amazon.com/-/es/Analytic-Production-Managers-Intelligence-Business/dp/0979888042

CHAPTER 9
Anticipating Humanitarian Crises and Challenges

The exact timing, impacts, and ramifications of unexpected catastrophic natural disasters, plagues, and conflicts cannot be predicted too far in advance, but they can be anticipated. These disasters and crises cannot be traced back to a single cause that can be prevented but are the result of a long-term combination of conditions, catalysts, drivers and triggers. **Warnings go unheeded, actions have unintended consequences, and some results are inevitable.** Disasters and crises are no longer confined to definable geographic regions but have global impacts and international repercussions.

In the past, catastrophic natural disasters, plagues, genocides and regional wars have devastated humanity but were largely contained to definable geographic areas. However, as the world has become more **inter-connected and entangled**, natural, human, and technological threats can potentially have cataclysmic human, economic, social, and environmental global impacts. There are also potential threats that are becoming more likely: the intentional or accidental use of nuclear weapons, a cyber-shutdown of global critical infrastructure, the spread of a natural mutation or bioengineered pathogen.

Swans, Rhinos, Frogs and Dragons

Four animalistic metaphors have been used to represent surprise events:

Black Swan: Popularized by Nassim Nicholas Taleb in 2011, Black Swans **are rare, unexpected events that have catastrophic effects.** A Black Swan event may have happened in the past, like a pandemic, but it catches the affected community off guard and has a significant impact on the human population.

In contrast, **Gray Rhinos**, introduced by Michele Wucker in 2013, are **highly probable events but they are neglected** until they occur, having devastating effects on the population. The linkage between the change in global climate and the increased frequency of storms, floods, droughts, heatwaves and wildfires has scientific evidence. However, it is still denied and ignored by many in the international community, which has not taken sufficient steps to address it.

Somewhat similar are **Boiling Frogs**, which describes conditions or situation that gradually gets worse until it reaches **a tipping point trigger of catastrophic proportions**. Slow-onset disasters and conflicts tend to receive less attention from humanitarian decision makers until they reach a threshold point that generates more severe impacts. Humanitarian priorities change as new disasters and conflicts emerge that receive more media attention and more resource allocations.

Dragon King, a concept developed by Didier Sornnete, is **an extreme outlier event** that has global cataclysmic impacts. It may what Clarke and Eddy call it an "initial Occurrence" that has never happened before, at least not in generational cultural memory, such as use of nuclear weapons, critical infrastructure cyber shutdown, bio-engineered pandemic, asteroid strike, etc. The international community is completely unprepared for such a cataclysmic dragon king event. It is a **game changer**, like dragons in Game of Thrones.

ANIMALISTIC METAPHORS FOR UNANTICIPATED EVENTS

Four animal metaphors can be used to describe surprise humanitarian crises:[65]

- Black Swans are rare unanticipated catastrophes, such as a pandemic.
- Gray Rhinos are probable, but neglected, threats that become high-impact disasters, such as a super typhoon.
- Boiling Frogs are slow, long-simmering humanitarian crises that eventually become a humanitarian catastrophe.
- Dragon Kings are extreme first-time cataclysmic events, such as the use of nuclear weapons, a critical transnational cyber shutdown, sea level rise, or an astronomical phenomenon that affects Earth (e.g. solar storm; asteroid, meteorite, comet strike.)[66]

Prediction vs. Anticipation

There is a definitional distinction between prediction and anticipation: **prediction identifies, describes, and forecasts events**, conditions or probable outcomes that might be expected to exist months and even years ahead. **Anticipation foresees and warns about emerging conditions, trends, threats, and opportunities** that may require a rapid shift in posture, priorities, or preparation. It is more about exploring scenarios and possibilities than predicting the timing of future events.

The problems of predictive analysis can be personified by three characters from ancient Greek Literature:

Cassandra, from Homer Iliad (8th Century BC) was the Trojan princess and priestess, who was given the gift of prophecy by the god Apollo. However, after she spurned Apollo's sexual advances, he put a curse on her that no one would believe her prophecies. When the Trojans would not heed her warning about the Trojan Horse and brought it inside the walls of the city, it resulted in the Greek military takeover of Troy. The Greeks captured and killed Cassandra after their victory over the Trojans.

The Boy who Cried Wolf, from Aesop's Fables (6th Century BC) is the story of a young shepherd boy whose job was to warn and guard against wolf attacks on the village flock, but he repeatedly makes false alarms about wolf attacks that fools the villagers until they eventually start to ignore him. Then, a pack of wolves really does attack the flock, killing and eating the sheep and the shepherd boy.

Finally, **Oedipus Rex** (Sophocles 5th Century BC), is the play about a young man who encounters the Delphic Oracle, which informs him that he will kill his real father and marry his real birth mother. Despite knowing this prophecy, he mistakenly kills his father, who is the King of Thebes, on the road to Thebes. Later, Oedipus saves the city of Thebes from the Sphinx and becomes the king of Thebes and marries the former king's widow, who is really his mother. When he later learns that he fulfilled the oracle's prophecy without knowing it, he gouges his eyes out.

In all three cases, the prophecies did not end well for the three characters.

The three stories serve as lessons for predictive analysis:

- **Cassandra** – no matter how hard you try; people will not believe your warnings.

- **Boy who Cried Wolf** – if your predictions do not come true after several specific warnings, people will stop believing you.

- **Oedipus Rex** – you cannot prevent a prediction from coming true and you may even inadvertently fulfill the prediction, even though you had the warning in advance.

UNFORESEEN CONSEQUENCES AND PREDICTION FAILURES: LESSONS FROM ANCIENT GREEK LITERATURE

In Homer's Iliad (8th century BC), the Trojan prophetess, Cassandra, was condemned to utter true prophecies but never to be believed. After she prophesized the fall of Troy, vengeful Greeks killed her. One of Aesop's fables, "The Boy Who Cried Wolf" (6th century BC) tells the story of a shepherd boy whose repeated false alarms about a wolf attacking the village flock cause the villagers to stop believing him, until one day the wolves attack the flock and eat the sheep and the shepherd boy. In Sophocles play *Oedipus Rex* (5th century BC), a young Oedipus is told by the Delphi Oracle that he will marry his birth mother and murder his father. He becomes King of Thebes, but later learns that despite knowing the prophecy, he unwittingly did both, and he then gouges his eyes out. In all three cases, the predictions did not end well.

READINGS AND REFERENCES

Dennis King, **Channeling Cassandra: Humanitarian Intelligence and Decision making in the Age of Complexity**. National Intelligence University, November 2024 https://www.ni-u.edu/wp-content/uploads/2024/11/NIUMonographKing2024_DNI_2024_04334.pdf

Niall Ferguson. **Gray Rhinos, Black Swans and Dragon Kings: Of Wars and Pandemics**. Hoover Institute, Stanford University. May 2020. https://www.hoover.org/sites/default/files/research/docs/dragon_kings_2020_05_02_final1.pdf

Niall Ferguson. **Doom: The Politics of Catastrophe**, New York, Penguin Press, 2021.

Dennis J. King

CHAPTER 10
Case Studies on Surprise Events

One thing that history has taught us is that despite our advances in science, technology and intelligence techniques, **we have not become any better at predicting, mitigating or preventing natural mega-disasters or armed conflicts.** The international community often ignores warnings of devastating impacts as the result of impending natural or environmental catastrophes, pandemic outbreaks, mass atrocities, terrorist attacks, or fast-onset conflicts.

Previous unanticipated or ignored humanitarian crises and disruptions

Humanitarian Dysfunction (2025) One dramatic disruption that occurred in 2025 should have been anticipated – the current disruption and dysfunction of the international humanitarian system. Over the past several years, the traditional system has become overstretched – widening gaps between humanitarian needs and provided resources, the prolonged non-resolution of conflict-driven crises, and increased frequency and severity of climate change-driven disasters. However, perhaps the most significant disruption were the changes enacted by the Trump the Second administration that reconfigured the U.S. foreign aid structure, drastically reduced the humanitarian funding of the previous largest government aid donor, and has had a cascading impact on the entire international humanitarian system.

Syria (2024) The conflict against Bashir al-Assad's regime began in 2011 and by 2024 the international community was experiencing fatigue, apathy and frustration with the on-going humanitarian crisis.

Over 13 years, the Syrian regime's military attacks against non-government-controlled territory drove 6 million Syrian refugees to other countries and displaced 7.4 million out of the total 17 million in need of humanitarian aid inside the country. In December 2024, following the retraction of Russian, Iranian, and Hezbollah military support to the regime, the anti-Assad rebel forces quickly took over Damascus and Bashir Al-Assad fled to Russia.

Gaza Strip (2023) The 7 October 2023 Hamas cross-border attack, massacre and abductions caught Israeli and U.S. intelligence by surprise, despite some signs and indicators. This was also true of the international humanitarian community, which had minimal number of humanitarian organizations on the ground providing mostly education, health, shelter and food assistance usually in coordination with Hamas authorities. Israeli retaliatory airstrikes, ground troop invasion, and disruption of logistical access resulted in over 2 million internally displaced and in need of humanitarian assistance.

Libya (2023) In September 2023, a meteorologically atypical tropical storm hit the eastern coast of Libya. The cities of Benghazi, Al Marj, Al Bayda, Sousa, and Derna experienced extreme winds, heavy rain and massive flooding from the collapse of two dams. Between 6,000 and 11,000 people were reported dead or missing and over 250,000 were targeted for UN humanitarian assistance. As a result of ongoing civil war, two different governments have controlled the country since March 2022, the Tripoli-based and internationally recognized Government of National Unity, which controls the western part of the country and the Government of National Stability, which controls the central and eastern part of Libya.

Sudan (2023) A new civil war between two major rival factions of the military government of Sudan: the Sudanese Armed Forces (SAF) and the paramilitary Rapid Support Forces (RSF) and its allies the Janjaweed coalition began during Ramadan on 15 April 2023.

Sudan experienced civil wars, political coups, and secessionist conflicts since the 1970s and 80s. This most recent conflict has led to a designation of famine in some areas, mass civilian casualties and displacement, entanglements by other countries, and reports of ethnic cleansing, disease outbreaks, and sexual violence atrocities. In October 2025, the RSF captured the city of El Fasher from the SAF and massacred thousands of civilians and caused mass displacement and starvation (IPC Phase 5 Famine).

Turkey/Syria Earthquakes (2023) On 6 February 2023, two earthquakes, both over 7.5, struck southern and central Turkey, also affecting northern and western Syria. The mega-disaster killed over 50,000 people in Turkey, including over 6,500 Syrian refugees, as well as other refugees from Iraq and Afghanistan. An estimated 6,000 people in Syria were killed. Over 5 million people in Turkey and approximately 5 million in Syria were targeted for international humanitarian assistance, many of these also affected and displaced by Syria's civil war. The UN and the rest of the international humanitarian community had to deal with two different governance structures: the Turkish national and provincial authorities and the anti-Assad, rebel structures in northern Syria. The UN issued two separate flash appeals: $1 billion for Turkey and almost $400 million for Syria in both rebel and government-controlled areas.

Ukraine (2022) Russia's obvious mass military build-up on its border with Ukraine in late 2021 was thought by many to be a Putin military bluff and posturing. However, in February 2022 Russia launched a full-scale military land invasion from Russian-controlled territory in eastern Ukraine, as well as from the north and an attempt to take over Kyiv. Russian airstrikes targeted critical infrastructure, urban civilian areas and health facilities throughout the country. As of the end of 2025, the armed conflict situation on the ground is mostly at a stalemate and almost 6 million Ukrainian refugees are in neighboring countries and nearly 4 million are internally displaced and/or in need of humanitarian aid.

Afghanistan (2021). The withdrawal of U.S. military forces began in May 2021, as part of a 2020 negotiated deal with the Taliban, and was completed by the end of August 2021. The withdrawal triggered the quicker-than-expected collapse of the Afghan Nation Security Forces, which led to Taliban takeover of Kabul in mid-August. Although active conflict subsided as the Taliban gained control of the entire country, almost half of the population – some 22.9 million people – require humanitarian assistance with 14.8 million people, more than one-third of the population, facing acute food insecurity.

Pandemic (2020) The worst contagion pandemic in over 100 years caught the international community off-guard and unprepared. Coronavirus-19 (COVID-19) emerged in late 2019 and still has a publicly undetermined origin. By the end of 2024, a reported total number of deaths worldwide was over 7 million and there were over 775 million reported cases, although both these numbers are undercounted. Despite the history of pandemics and improved epidemiological monitoring, COVID-19 caught the world unprepared and changed the way we live, work, socialize and cope with a pervasive infectious disease. The definitive origin of the Coronavirus is still officially a "known unknown" and is still being debated.

READINGS AND REFERENCES

Dennis King. **20/20 Hindsight: the precursors of the current humanitarian chaos.** LinkedIn, 26 May 2025 **https://www.linkedin.com/pulse/2020-hindsight-precursors-current-humanitarian-chaos-dennis-king-vnmye/**

Al Jazeera. **What happened in Syria? How did al-Assad fall?** Al Jazeera. 8 December 2024. **https://www.aljazeera.com/news/2024/12/8/what-happened-in-syria-has-al-assad-really-**

fallen

Martin Indyk. **Why Hamas Attacked—and Why Israel Was Taken by Surprise.** Foreign Affairs. 7 October 2023. https://www.foreignaffairs.com/middle-east/martin-indyk-why-hamas-attacked-and-why-israel-was-taken-surprise

Tammy Webber. **Cyclone that devastated Libya is latest extreme event with some hallmarks of climate change.** Independent, 12 September 2023. https://www.independent.co.uk/news/ap-libya-mediterranean-greece-university-of-maryland-b2410219.html

UN Office for the Coordination of Humanitarian Affairs (OCHA). **The Sudan conflict: What's really going on.** OCHA, 21 February 2025. https://www.unocha.org/news/sudan-conflict-whats-really-going

Scripps Institution of Oceanography. **The Unexpected Physics Behind Turkey's Devastating 2023 Earthquakes.** UC San Diego, 03 August 2023. https://scripps.ucsd.edu/news/unexpected-physics-behind-turkeys-devastating-2023-earthquakes

Francois Grunewald, **Real-Time Evaluation of the Humanitarian Response to the Crisis Resulting from the War in Ukraine.** *Groupe URD,* "August 28, 2022, https://reliefweb.int/report/ukraine/real-time-evaluation-humanitarian-response-ukraine-july-24th-august-18th-2022

Congressional Research Service. **U.S. Military Withdrawal and Taliban Takeover in Afghanistan: Frequently Asked Questions.** CRS, 20 August 2021. https://www.congress.gov/crs_external_products/R/PDF/R46879/R46879.1.pdf

Associated Press. **Origins of COVID-19 still unclear, according to final report from WHO expert group.** AP. 17 June 2025. https://www.cbc.ca/news/health/covid-19-origins-report-1.7572830

Dennis J. King

CHAPTER 11
Making the Humanitarian System Smarter

The key to making humanitarian decisions more effective is making the humanitarian system smarter. This does not only relate to the international network and processes of external humanitarian actors (UN agencies, INGOs, donors), but also to the national and local community actors. While it is useful, AI alone is not the solution to making the humanitarian system smarter. Keeping human beings **responsible and accountable** for making decisions that lead to actions that save lives, alleviate suffering, restore livelihoods and infrastructure, and establish security and stability, needs to be the refocus of the humanitarian community.

Localized decision making

Obviously, the nation affected by a natural disaster suffers the greatest impact, has the greatest interest, and bears the greatest responsibility for addressing the emergency needs of the population and ensuring future progress. It is the national and local governments, communities and civil society organizations that are the first responders to the people in immediate need; providing search and rescue, emergency medical trauma care, the provision of shelter, food, water and sanitation, and health services to those who need it.

Over the years, a paternalistic international system of international aid organizations, donor governments, foreign-based NGOs and charities, and expatriates has dominated emergency operations and services, perpetuating dependency and their continued presence and control. In recent years, a new buzzword - **"localization"** has become accepted, but it is not donors and international organizations simply sub-contracting on-the-ground response work to national and local actors. Real localization is transferring and empowering national actors to make operational response decisions, especially for natural disaster events.

The 2025 humanitarian funding collapse and humanitarian system dysfunction forced a **"reset, reorganization, and revitalization"** of the international humanitarian system and network, including the necessity of localization and enhancement of accountability, greater crisis management capability, and informed decision making at the national and local level.

Providing these actors with their own advanced technological tools (GIS, satellite imagery, robotics, AI) that can be used to enhance analysis and decision making is needed. However, this also includes challenges:

Infrastructure constraints – AI requires advanced technological infrastructure, which may not be consistent or adequate in the affected country. This infrastructure can be disrupted by disaster, conflict or cyberattack.

Digital Divide – although the divide is closing, there still exists a chasm between countries and populations who have access, connectivity, technical skills, affordable equipment, and familiarity with computers and the internet and those who don't. This is especially true of AI.

Language bias – AI is derived from available content on the internet, which is heavily dominated by English and other major language text and does not capture many indigenous languages, diverse dialects, or tacit knowledge.

Cultural bias – AI systems are trained on vast datasets that reflect or perpetuate the values and norms of specific dominant cultures and marginalize alternative mindsets.

Whether **it is intentional or not**, the more AI is integrated into the humanitarian system, the more that actors from advanced countries will likely remain dominant.

The first step is ensuring that affected host countries have access to early warning systems, technologies (satellite imagery, AI, coordination networking applications, etc.) needed to make decisions for their own response operations, preparedness planning, and longer-term recovery and stabilization. Without access to available data, information and analysis translated into their national language, national/local government and civil society organizations cannot assume more control and responsibility over emergency operations and addressing the humanitarian needs of their own people.

The international community does have a role to play, not only in providing **pooled funding** to country-based relief and rehabilitation projects, but also sharing anticipatory analysis, lessons learned and best practices from other responses and assisting coordination with international actors and neighboring countries that may be impacted. The objective of empowering national actors to be **self-sufficient** can only be achieved by providing these actors with the data, information and analysis real-time and in their own language to make operational decisions.

International Humanitarian Intelligence Unit

Part of the problem is that decision makers are overwhelmed by the overload of information, increasing uncertainty, competing sources and systems, and the ineffective presentation that prevents making provided analysis actionable. New and improved, remote and removed proprietary platforms are not enough to **channel actionable**

intelligence to decision makers. These tools, systems and platforms can be useful to humanitarian analysts that work for and are accountable to identified decision makers, but they are not the ultimate solution in addressing the current humanitarian challenges.

In their book **"Warnings: Finding Cassandras to Stop Catastrophes"**, Richard A. Clarke and R.P Eddy propose an institutional system or unit to provide intelligence support to decision makers – one that has a team relationship with the decision makers that establishes direct access, trust, and accountability. Back in 2000, the Report of the Panel on United Nations Peace Keeping Operations (UNPKO), commonly called **the Brahimi Report**, recommended the creation of a new information-gathering and analysis entity to support the informational and analytical needs of the Secretary-General. However, lack of Member State support to embedding an "intelligence" function inside the United Nations prevented any official establishment of such a function at UN PKO.

Such a humanitarian intelligence service would need to be independent and not embedded in any single humanitarian operational or programmatic agency. It could perform the following functions:

- Tasked to answer specific questions
- Tasked to investigate and report on specific problems
- Scan the horizon for potential/anticipated threats and risks
- Provide Deep Dive briefings – monitor ongoing crises
- Develop Encrypted secret scenarios and contingency plans

There are different options for creating such an entity:

- A centrally managed **consortium of think tanks**, academic and research institutions, field partners, etc. providing briefings, interactive dashboards, and issue papers to decision makers.

- Joint intelligence **situation room/center** with a 24/7 team monitoring and forwarding critical information to decision makers

- A human staffed and AI facilitated **Knowledge hub** that filters, highlights, streamlines and evaluates critical information and analysis to provide directly to decision makers

- A **decision support secretariat** to an executive committee such as the Inter-Agency Steering Committee or the National Security Council

- An official **crisis warning office or team** dedicated to assessing, foreseeing, anticipating, and mitigating and/or thwarting humanitarian risks and threats

- An **advisory board** of subject matter experts and former senior officials providing guidance and recommendations to a current decision-making body.

In the full disclosure, I was an original member of a both classified and open-source team at the U.S. Department of State, in the Bureau of Intelligence and Research, called the Humanitarian Information Unit (HIU). I decided to retire after 20 years at the State Department in May 2024 and the HIU was disbanded later that year. In my personal perspective, the unit failed because it was not respected or appreciated inside INR and the broader U.S. intelligence community, it was ignored and distrusted by the U.S Government humanitarian offices, and it was not valued for its potential utility. Overcoming bureaucratic resistance, suspicion, and rivalry from already established offices and projects will be a significant challenge in the formation of such an **independent, neutral international entity**.

READINGS AND REFERENCES

Richard A. Clarke and R.P Eddy**. Warnings: Finding Cassandras to Stop Catastrophes.** Ecco, May 2017. https://www.amazon.com/Warnings-Finding-Cassandras-Stop-Catastrophes/dp/ 0062488023

William J. Durch et al. **The Brahimi Report and the Future of UN Peace Operations.** The Stimson Center, 2003. https://www.stimson.org/wp-content/files/file-attachments/BR-CompleteVersion-Dec03_1.pdf

Dennis J. King

CHAPTER 12
Recommendations for the Analyst and Decision Maker

Recommendations for the Analyst

The job of the analyst is to make judgments when faced with unknowns, uncertainty and unpredictability. The position of humanitarian affairs analyst is not recognized or designated in most humanitarian organizations. Now that I am retired, I am passing on **ten recommendations to an analyst specializing in humanitarian issues**:

Be Accountable for your analysis

- Include source citations and credibility, levels of confidence and probability, caveats, and necessary disclaimers.

Make analysis actionable

- Identify the actions that need to be taken, the questions that need to be answered, the obstacles that need to be overcome.

Keep the analysis short and focused

- Do not tell the decision makers what they want to hear, tell them what they already know, or tell them what they don't need to know.

Tailor the presentation to the needs, preferences and pressures of the decision maker

- In the first paragraph of a written analysis or the first minute of analytical briefing, explain to the intended audience what to expect and the value and key judgments of the product or presentation.

Solicit peer review for your assumptions, conclusions, and recommendations before presentation to decision makers.

- Consider alternative judgments, opposing viewpoints, and external ground truthing.

Avoid political advocacy in your analysis.

- Keep advocacy and analysis separate. Avoid venting, political emotionalism, one-sided perspective, subjective judgements, and personal conflicts of interest that will detract from the objectivity of analysis.

Don't assume that the intended audience thinks like you do.

- or has the esoteric knowledge that you have or considered the different perspectives.

Recognize AI's benefits and limitations for your research.

- AI can filter, extract, summarize on-line data and information amazingly fast, but cannot capture tacit knowledge, known unknowns, and personal experience.

Be objective and not just dedicated to making the decision maker "look good" or following groupthink consensus.

- Represent the interests of the humanitarian community and the affected populations to provide an alternative to an opposing political, military, or economic self-interest perspective.

Seek feedback and evaluation.

- Solicit after-action review and feedback from your target audience, although decision makers are often reluctant to evaluate the intelligence input or their decision/actions.

Recommendations for the Decision Maker

While humanitarian analysts and subject matter experts may be long-term personnel of a humanitarian organization, decision makers may be political, with fixed term appointments on rotation. By nature, most decision and policy makers tend to be optimists, committed to making things happen, extremely busy and preoccupied, and have short attention spans.

Be Accountable for your decisions.

- Recognize which actions are under your control and which are not, take responsibility for your decisions that led to actions and the positive or negative outcomes and effects.

Try to find out the decisions and planned responses of other humanitarian actors in advance.

- So, you can possibly combine funding and coordinate synergistic efforts to avoid duplication of activities.

Try not to make counterproductive decisions.

- Don't burn bridges, alienate key partners, or undermine longer-term strategic goals.

Make decisions on things that your organizations can influence and can have impact.

- Avoid making decisions and taking actions that are doomed to fail.

Understand the motivations of your decisions.

- Before making the final decision, acknowledge to yourself the pressures, influences, and personal benefits of making the decision.

Sometimes, the decision is not to act.

- Analysis may suggest that no action is necessary or action at this time is premature or might be counterproductive.

Establish a relationship with your support staff, analysts and advisors.

- Ask them for the information you are seeking and for answers to your specific questions. Convey your priorities, preferences and problems so they can anticipate your analytical needs.

Engage with the analysis/analyst.

- Feel free to question, challenge and play devil's advocate.

To deal with overload, filter the most critical material you need to make decisions.

- Rely on trusted individuals, team, subscription mailing lists, or personally tailored search engines to filter the published resources you need to review.

When at first you don't succeed – Plan B.

When things outside your control sabotage your decisions and actions, have a contingency plan option.

READINGS AND REFERENCES

Center for the Study of Intelligence. **Intelligence Support to the Senior Working Levels of Policy: Lessons from Experienced Practitioners.** Center for the Study of Intelligence. January 2014

APPENDIX 1
Analysis of Survey Analysis

Following my own recommended best practices,

- I sought external input from other individuals with diverse experiences and backgrounds.
- I identified biases in my methodology
- I identified caveats and disclaimers

Many people don't like to take on-line surveys, including me. Within my requested timeframe, I got 35 respondents to the survey I posted on SurveyMonkey.

Analysis for Humanitarian Decision Making

Ranking of challenges to using analysis for decision making? (Top 5)

Challenge	Percentage
Bias (politicization, confirmation, groupthink)	70%
Knowledge Gaps and Unknowns	63%
Overload	55%
Siloed, circular or status quo thinking	55%

Not actionable - not provided in time to act upon	49%
Out-of-Date	42%
Can't verify or trust source	30%
Lack of early warning-anticipation	27%
Misinformation/Disinformation	21%
Conflicting Analysis	21%

Ranking of personal preferences for receiving information/analysis

Format	Ranking
Written (assessments, evaluations, analysis)	4.48
Visual (maps, graphs, charts, imagery, photos)	4.24
Group Interactive	4.06
Deep Dive Briefings	3.85
Personal Interactive	3.19
AI Q&A Chatbot	1.30

Ranking of preferred sources of information

Source	Ranking
United Nations or other international organizations	1
Non-Governmental Organizations	2
Your organization's internal information	3
Traditional News Media	4
Academia & Research Think Tanks	5
Affected person interviews/surveys	6
Governments (Donors and Host Governments	7
Commercial Vendors/Providers (subscription, purchased)	8
Social media feeds	9

Respondents

To take the survey, I selected people I know or am familiar with who held operational, programmatic and/or strategic decision-making positions in humanitarian organizations. This is a selection bias.

Ranking the type of decision making you engage in

Type of Decision Making	Ranking
Strategic/Policy	2.64
Programmatic/Funding	1.85
Operational/response	1.52

Ranking of Type of humanitarian organization have you worked for? (multiple choice)

Type of Organization	Responses
Donor Government	27
Non-Governmental Organization	23
UN or international organization	16
Academic/Research Think Tank	7
Local Community Organization	1
Military	1

What level is/was your position?

Level	Count
Senior – Top three levels -Head, Deputy or Assistant Director - 22	22
Mid-Level – manager, unit chief, officer - 10	11

Where did you primarily work?

Location	Percentage
at organization headquarters	48%
in the field – crisis affected countries	15%
almost equally in the field and at headquarters	36%

Humanitarian Portfolios

The humanitarian sector is diverse and multi-thematic, with many overlapping and inter-connected disciplines.

Ranking your focus areas? (your Top 5)

Thematic/Sectoral Portfolio	Responses	Percent
Conflict – Stabilization	24	72%
Humanitarian Funding/Disaster management	23	70%
Displacement/Migration/Shelter	21	63%
Humanitarian Security/Access	17	52%
Natural Disasters/Hazards	12	36%
Disease/Health	12	36%
Climate Change/Environment	11	34%

Local Resilience/Empowerment	10	30%
Food Security	8	24%
Children (health, education)	7	21%
Water/sanitation	6	18%
Gender	4	12%
Technology	2	6%
Other	6	18%

Geographic Portfolio

Geographic Focus	Percentage
Global – 47%	45%
Country/Region Specific	3%
Both	51%

APPENDIX 2
The Humanitarian Accidental Tourist

The Development Set- a poem by Ross Coggins, 1976

Excuse me, friends, I must catch my jet
I'm off to join the Development Set;
My bags are packed, and I've had all my shots
I have travelers' checks and pills for the trots!

The Development Set is bright and noble
Our thoughts are deep and our vision global;
Although we move with the better classes
Our thoughts are always with the masses.

In Sheraton Hotels in scattered nations
We damn multi-national corporations;
injustice seems easy to protest
In such seething hotbeds of social rest.

We discuss malnutrition over steaks
And plan hunger talks during coffee breaks.
Whether Asian floods or African drought,
We face each issue with open mouth.

We bring in consultants whose circumlocution
Raises difficulties for every solution --
Thus guaranteeing continued good eating
By showing the need for another meeting.

*The language of the Development Set
Stretches the English alphabet;
We use swell words like "epigenetic"
"Micro", "macro", and "logarithmetic"*

*It pleasures us to be esoteric --
It's so intellectually atmospheric!
And although establishments may be unmoved,
Our vocabularies are much improved.*

*When the talk gets deep and you're feeling numb,
You can keep your shame to a minimum:
To show that you, too, are intelligent
Smugly ask, "Is it really development?"*

*Or say, "That's fine in practice, but don't you see:
It doesn't work out in theory!"
A few may find this incomprehensible,
But most will admire you as deep and sensible.*

*Development set homes are extremely chic,
Full of carvings, curios, and draped with batik.
Eye-level photographs subtly assure
That your host is at home with the great and the poor.*

*Enough of these verses - on with the mission!
Our task is as broad as the human condition!
Just pray god the biblical promise is true:
The poor ye shall always have with you.*

I came across this Ross Coggins poem when I started my humanitarian career in the late 1980s. My first "real job" was as a humanitarian information officer at USAID's Office of U.S. Foreign Disaster Assistance, writing reports and sometimes deployed as a member of a Disaster Assistance Response Team sent by the US Government to a disaster-affected country. When I was on those teams, I worked out of the US Embassy or USAID Mission in the national capital, stayed in expensive tourist hotels, and occasionally went on short field assessments to disaster affected areas. After

USAID, I got employment with UN Office for Coordination of Humanitarian Affairs' ReliefWeb project and later with UNICEF, based in New York and Geneva. In 2002, I was asked to join the newly created Humanitarian Information Unit at the U.S. Department of State in Washington DC, where I worked until retirement in 2024.

When I started my humanitarian career thirty-five years ago, the humanitarian profession was just beginning an employment boom. The humanitarian role of the US Agency for International Development and U.S. State Department was expanding, the UN agency bureaucracy and field presence was growing, and the number of international NGOs was proliferating. Humanitarian job vacancy platforms were created (ReliefWeb, DEVEX, LinkedIn, etc.) Not only did the need for field-deployed aid workers increase, but a whole new type of tech-savvy ICT specialist (GIS specialists, data scientists, website managers and editors, etc.) was being recruited to adapt to the innovation. Given the ever-increasing humanitarian needs, the sector has become a growth industry.

Now the humanitarian profession is experiencing an employment bust. Upon taking office in January 2025, the Trump the Second administration immediately implemented its plan to abolish the U.S. Agency for International Development and rescind 83% of its humanitarian and development funding. Within six months, the Administration fired 1,600 USAID government employees and transferred selected USAID functions and programs to the State Department. In addition to the fired USAID employees, the Trump II Administration fired 1,300 State Department foreign service officer and civil service employees. Furthermore, the cancellation of USAID-funded projects administered by UN agencies, NGOs, and private sector contractors laid off thousands of employees and aid workers, having a cascading calamitous effect on the entire international humanitarian system. This has created an extremely competitive labor pool of very experienced humanitarian professionals. The total number of vacancy postings have fallen by around 25% on the DEVEX job board in 2025.

Now that I am retired, can write what I want to write, and have minimal stakes in the future, I can speculate on the future trends in the humanitarian profession.

First, local hires will assume the professional functions of many positions in humanitarian organizations that were held by expatriates from the Global North and West. Not only do local hires have the experience, expertise and education/training credentials now more than ever before, their salaries and expenses are far less of a cost to employer humanitarian organization's budgets. The localization of the humanitarian profession will increase the accountability and responsibility of the local and national actors for the humanitarian effects in their own country.

Second, the advances and promotion of Artificial Intelligence tools and systems have already started to revolutionize the humanitarian profession, aided by the financial backing and innovation of some of the biggest tech companies in the world. As humanitarian organization bureaucrats have been laid off in the recent employment bust, AI has begun taking over many professional roles, including data/information collection, routine report writing, on-line training, program accounting and management, metrics monitoring and evaluation and routine administrative functions. In addition, a whole new generation of professionals dedicated to the promotion of AI applications has been established in the humanitarian sector.

However, there are many jobs that I can't imagine being replaced by AI or robots, such as hands-on health professionals, emergency paramedics, water and sanitation system engineers, shelter providers, security officers, on-site assessment specialists, etc. Saving human lives and serving the needs of humanity should remain the ultimate responsibility of humanity, so that we remain accountable. Hopefully, there will still be jobs for human subject matter analysts and humanitarian decision makers to provide a personal check and counterbalance on AI.

Finally, as Boomers and Gen X professionals retire, Millennials and Gen Z will replace them, especially in senior-level positions in humanitarian organizations. These professionals have entirely different technical skills, work experience, and lifestyle culture than the previous generations. These technocrats may be far more susceptible to AI and social media influencers for insight on humanitarian issues than on advisors, educators, print journalists, subject matter specialists, or writers like me.

http://shores-system.mysite.com/development_set.html

INDEX

Accountability – 5, 40-42, 56-57, 59, 62, 64, 76
Anticipation – 2, 3, 6-7, 21, 25-26, 28, 30, 40, 43, 45, 37, 50, 58-60
Artificial Intelligence or AI – 16, 19, 28, 34-38, 42, 76

Bias – 2, 3, 39, 57-58, 67, 69
"Black Swans" – 45-46
"Boiling Frogs" – 45-46
Bottom Line Up Front (BLUF) – 1, 32, 43
Boy Who Cried Wolf (Aesop) – 48-49
Brahimi Report – 59, 61

Cassandra – 42, 47-49, 59, 61
Country-Based Pooled Funds (CBPF) – 15-17
COVID-19 – 53, 55
Cynefin Framework: Complicated, Complex, Chaos - 5

Dichotomy of Control – 18, 22
Diplomacy – 6, 13-15, 21, 23-24,
Disinformation – 3, 20, 39, 41, 68
"Dragon Kings" – 45-47, 49

Famine Early Warning System (FEWS) – 25, 28

Gaza Conflict – 13-15, 17, 20, 39, 42, 51
Groupthink – 2, 3, 20, 64, 67
"Gray Rhinos" – 45-46, 49

Humanitarian Intelligence: A Practitioner's Guide to Crisis Analysis and Project Design (Andrej Zwitter) – 23, 28-29

Humanitarian Intelligence – 19-20, 23-24, 26-28, 30-32, 43, 58-59

Integrated Phase Classification (IPC) – 14, 25-26, 28, 52

Iraq Conflict – 16, 20, 52

Libya Storm (2023) – 51, 54

Oedipus Rex **(Sophocles)** – 48-49
Operational/Response Decision-Making – 6, 10-13, 16, 34. 57-58

Prediction – 28, 30, 37, 41, 45, 47-48, 50
Programmatic/Funding Decision-Making – 6, 8, 13, 15-16, 70

Strategic/Policy Decision-Making – 6-7, 13-15, 70
Structured Analytic Techniques – 26, 28
Sudan Conflict – 52, 54
Syria Conflict – 51, 52, 54

Turkey/Syria Earthquake (2023) – 52, 54

Ukraine conflict – 20, 23, 52-54

Warnings: Finding Cassandras to Stop Catastrophes **(Richard A. Clarke and R.P Eddy) 2017** – 46, 59, 61

Yemen Conflict – 13-14, 16

Dennis J. King

ABOUT THE AUTHOR

Dennis King has over 30 years' experience in the international humanitarian sector, starting at the U.S. Agency for International Development (USAID), then with the UN Office for Coordination of Humanitarian Affairs (UN OCHA) and the start-up of the Relief Web project in 1996 and finally working as a humanitarian affairs analyst at the U.S. Department of State until his retirement in 2024.

As a humanitarian affairs analyst at the U.S. State Department's Bureau of Intelligence and Research (INR) from 2002 - 2024, he provided written and graphic products, both classified and unclassified, to senior U.S. Government policy and decision makers on such humanitarian crises as Gaza, Ukraine, Syria, Sudan, Haiti, etc., as well as global issues such as aid worker security, the international humanitarian system, and anticipatory analysis.

www.ingramcontent.com/pod-product-compliance
Lightning Source LLC
Chambersburg PA
CBHW040222220526
45473CB00001B/89